The Gullahs
of South Carolina

Pearce W. Hammond

Halftide Publishing
Okatie, South Carolina 29909

The Gullahs
of South Carolina

ISBN-13: 978-0615486482

Library of Congress Control Number: 2011929319

Art, Text & Design: Pearce W. Hammond
Cover Design and Photography: Pearce W. Hammond

Published in the United States by
Halftide Publishing
20 Bellinger Cove
Okatie, South Carolina 29909

10-28-14

To John —

Always Remember the
good times we had
and stay young at heart.
Best Regards,

Pearce

This book is affectionately dedicated to my wife
Anne Hancock Hammond
whose support and encouragement made this work possible.

Contents

Preface

When I was a young boy in the early 1950's, one of my most pleasant and significant memories of the Gullah/Geechee people was during a weekend fishing trip with my father and several of his friends to one of the remote sea islands off the coast of Georgia. We left Savannah and traveled down the intercoastal waterway to Blackbeard Island where we anchored behind the island in the mouth of Cabretta Inlet to go surf fishing. On the way we stopped at Raccoon Bluff on Sapelo Island which was a small fishing village inhabited by Geechees. When we arrived I felt like I was in an African village. The Geechee people were very friendly and you could tell that they were almost completely cut off from the outside world and were self-sufficient living off the land and the water and did not have to depend on others for their food and other needs. While we were there, we were invited to share some smoked Mullet with them. During the meal I had my first introduction into their unique Gullah/Geechee language which I found very difficult to understand. That unique experience at Raccoon Bluff on Sapelo Island has remained with me over the years and helped to spark my interest in learning more about their way of life and culture.

I had another experience with the Gullah people in the late 1950's when I went with my father to a Plantation in Yemassee, South Carolina to go duck hunting in the rice fields of the Combahee River. When we arrived at the hunting lodge, we were greeted by two elderly Gullah women, Bella and Essie, who prepared all of the meals, picked the ducks which were killed, and handled other chores for the members of the hunting club. I was again drawn to their unique language when they talked and sang while cooking meals on a wood stove in the kitchen. During that weekend one of the hunting club members celebrated a Birthday and I can still hear Bellie and Essie signing to him: "Hoppy, Hoppy Bird-day, Mr. Jak" as they brought the birthday cake to the dinner table.

Then there was Ely, an elderly Gullah man who arrived at 4 am each morning to build a fire in each room of the house to keep the hunters warm as they dressed and ate breakfast. Ely handled the boats and duck decoys and took the hunters and their dogs to their duck blinds in the old rice fields before sunrise. He was quite a character and I will never forget him and the Gullah language he spoke.

It was these two experiences I had as a young man which motivated me to learn more about the Gullah and Geechee people and their unique language and culture, and I hope that this work will inspire others to keep their story alive for future generations.

Introduction

My purpose in creating this work is to increase public awareness of the Gullah and Geechee culture and to pass along their story to future generations so they can recognize the significant contributions they have made to America's heritage.

The name "Gullah" may derive from Angola, a country in southwestern Africa where many of the Gullahs' ancestors originated. Some scholars have also suggested it comes from Gola, an ethnic group living on the border area between Sierra Leone and Liberia in Western Africa.

The Gullahs were former African slaves from the West African coastal countries of Senegal and Sierra Leone and settled on isolated sea islands and marsh areas between Wilmington, North Carolina and Jacksonville, Florida in the 19th Century. These islanders brought with them their ancestors' ability to cultivate rice along with many other traditional skills such as farming, fishing, basket making, net making, language, pottery, wood carvings and more. They lived in small farming and fishing communities and the climate and geographic isolation of the sea islands were integral to the development of their unique culture.

For generations their same peaceful way of life continued, filled with hard work but self-sufficiency and satisfaction. Fishermen flung their nets into creeks and ocean to catch crabs, shrimp, and fish, and gathered oysters and clams. Farmers hoed the sandy soil to grow vegetables and cotton. Winter was the time for sewing clothes and quilts and mending nets. Evenings and weekends were ideal for the telling of folktales, for basket making, for song and dance, and for the expression of religious faith and hope which united the people and reflected their African heritage.

In the Carolinas the culture is known as "Gullah" and in Florida and Georgia the culture is known as "Geechee". The name "Geechee" may come from Kissi (pronounced "Geezee"), a tribe living in the border area between Guinea, Sierra Leone, and Liberia.

Most of the Gullahs' ancestors were brought to South Carolina through the port of Charleston which was one of the most important ports in North America for the Atlantic slave trade, and almost half of the enslaved Africans came through the port of Charleston.

From their music and crafts, to religion and social customs, the Gullah and Geechee culture reflects important aspects of the African homeland.

Gullah-Geechee Cultural Heritage Corridor

Many Americans are unaware that along the South Carolina coast lies a culture more strongly rooted in African ways than any other in America. It was a time when most sea islanders were black and understood the importance of tucking Spanish moss into a shoe, painting window trim blue, and running like mad from a coachwhip snake. The rivers and ocean was theirs for fishing; the salt marshes theirs for shrimping, crabbing and

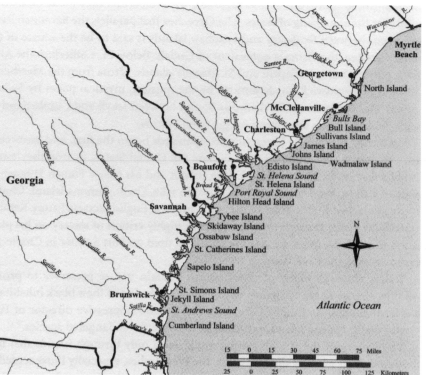

oystering; and the woods theirs for hunting. They sang spirituals and spoke their native tonque without shame. They wove baskets without worrying that the sweet grass might vanish from the swamps someday. They delivered their own babies, made medicine of herbs, and knitted their own fishing nets. They danced and clapped when they worshiped, told stories, and adorned graves with life's necessities and pleasures so the departed could pass easily and amiably between material and spirtual worlds.

In quiet self-sufficiency, the Gullahs lived off the water and the land and their unique culture thrived in isolation for centuries on the remote sea islands until the outside world discovered the islands and started paying millions to own them and new ways were forcing out the old. If Gullah dies, Gullah children won't know about the old lifestyle and a significant part of the culture of the low country will be lost along with African Americans' purest link to their past.

In 2006 the U.S. Congress passed the "Gullah/Geechee Cultural Heritage Corridor Act " that provides $10 million over ten years for the preservation and interpretation of historic sites relating to Gullah culture. The "heritage corridor" will extend from Jacksonville, Florida to Wilmington, North Carolina and the project will be administered by the U.S. National Park Service with strong input from the Gullah community.

The Gullah Language

Gullah Language

Forbidden by plantation owners to speak their own native tongue, the African slaves developed their own dialect out of necessity by incorporating broken English with African words. The Gullah language is a melodic blend of 17th and 18th century English and African dialects and was first spoken by slaves. It is still spoken by the Gullahs in the Carolinas and the Geechees in Georgia and Florida. The Gullah dialect survives today as a "creolized" version of English.The Gullah language attained creole status during the mid 1700s and was learned and used by the second generation of African Americans as their mother tonque. Growing from African roots, planted in American soil, and nourished by various English dialects, a linguistic analysis of the Gullah language will determine that the greater part of its lexicon is traceable to English words. However, the sentence structure, intonation, and stress reveal a clear correspondence to the languages spoken on the west coast of Africa.

Since Gullah is an English-derived creole, the English alphabet is used to represent its sounds. Most of the letters used in the spelling of Gullah words have the same sounds that are used to form English words. Gullah is a legitimate creole language and one that should be preserved as a significant part of our American heritage.

The following examples highlights some of the differences between Gullah and English:

"Hah hunnuh fah do"? - How are you?

"Hunnuh mus tek cyear ahde root fah heal de tree"! - You have to take care of the roots in order to heal the tree!

"Ef hunnuh ain kno weh hunnuh da from, hunnuh ain gwine kno weh hunnuh dey gwine"! - If you don't know where you are from, you won't know where you are going!

"Bwoy hunnuh betta cumyah befo mi jux yah"! - Boy you better come here before I whoop you!

"De Gullah gone a plowin een de fiel e fambly own and gone home tyad to de bone, bot him been good en glad." - The Gullah went plowing in the field his family owns and went home very tired but very glad.

The Gullah People

Seventy percent of the enslaved Africans who came to this country came ashore on the coast of South Carolina. These Africans brought with them a set of traditions, skills and beliefs that came to be known as the Gullah culture. It is a heritage so rich that no price tag can measure its value.

The Gullahs brought with them from Africa many of the skills needed to work the cotton, sugar, rice and tobacco plantations on the isolated sea islands.

Gullahs embrace a culture that honors God and country by fishing, hunting and gardening. However, with many of the sea islands now invaded by tourists, resort jobs have replaced fishing and farming and the traditional Gullah way of life is being swept away by modernization.

The Gullahs wove baskets, made medicine of herbs, delivered their own babies, and knitted their own fishing nets. They told stories, danced and clapped when they worshiped, adorned graves with conch shells, and warded off evil spirits with open bibles. In quiet self-sufficiency, they lived off the water and the land.

The Gullahs and Geechees lived in small farming and fishing communities on the remote sea islands. The climate and geographic isolation of the sea islands were integral to the development of their culture.

The Gullahs have a strong sense of community built on extended family units and have remained deeply connected to the roots of African culture.

On wash day Gullah women had to build a good hot fire and then keep the fire underneath the tub. The key to clean clothes in peaceful times gone by was plenty of elbow grease and plenty of rinsing.

Living from the Land

The Gullahs raised their own vegetables, planted their own corn and peas, and ground corn to make flour and grits. They killed hogs and cows for meat and went into the creeks and rivers for fish, crab, shrimp and to gather oysters and clams.

Living close to the land has long defined Gullah Culture.

"My daddy took me in de field and taught me 'bout using a Hoe when I was a little girl. I learned myself how to use dat Hoe and Ise used it tru de years."

Gullah farmers hoed the sandy soil to grow vegetables and cotton and for generations the same peaceful way of life continued. It was filled with hard work but also with self-sufficiency and satisfaction.

Among the many plants brought from Africa with the slave trade to the soil of South Carolina and Georgia were Okra, Benneseed, Cowpeas, Watermelon, Eggplant, and Peanuts.

"De Gullah gone a a plowin een de fiel e fambly own. Fus, e unhitch e hoss from weh hit beenna feedin all lone. Dat one lee hoss plow up all the dan de Gullah had. De Gullah gone home tyad to de bone, bot him been good en glad."

Translated: "The gullah went plowing in the field his family owns. First, he unhitched his horse from where it was feeding all alone. That one small horse plowed all the land the Gullah had. The Gullah went home very tired but very glad."

The sea islands off the coast of South Carolina, among them Edisto Island, Coosaw Island, Daufuskie Island, and St. Helena Island, have provided Gullah roots to millions of African Americans.

"*I work all de time from morning till late at night and never knowed what it was to rest. I had to do everything there was to do on de outside - work in de field, chop dat wood, hoe dat corn. I done everything except split dem rails.*"

Basket making is one of the nation's oldest art forms of African origin. Sea islanders wove baskets of sweet-smelling, pliable marsh grass to hold vegetables, cotton, shellfish and clothing. Today they make and sell these baskets to supplement their income.

Living from the Water

The myriad of waterways that wind around the sea islands made travel by boat a necessity for Gullahs from the earliest days of settlement and the abundance of fish, crab, shrimp and oysters provided food as well.

Oystering is a tradition of pride and hard work and for generations Gullah oystermen went out at low tide and harvested bushels of oysters.

Gullah oystermen went out during the "R" months of fall and winter in flat-bottomed wooden boats called "Bateaux" and harvested oysters from the river banks.

One oysterman could gather 60 to 100 bushels of oysters during a low tide and transport them to the oyster factory where they were steamed, shucked and canned.

Most of the Gullah oystermen who worked the rivers and gathered oysters are old or dead and their sons and grandsons have taken up other lines of work or have moved away. The Gullah oysterman on the river is nearing an end in our time.

The Gullah oysterman's boat was a rough-hewn, flat-bottomed wooden vessel known as a Bateau. These boats were rugged and river-worthy and their long wide shape was made to haul enormous loads of oysters.

Heavily laden with oysters in his flat bottomed wooden bateau, a Gullah oysterman heads back to the oyster factory.

Gullah oystermen wash down bushels of oysters on the docks at the oyster factory.

At the oyster factory shovel loads of oysters are heaved onto long cement tables where Gullah women use strong hands and small strong-tempered knives to open the shells, remove the oysters, and put them in steel pails.

The working tradition of the Gullah oystermen and women comes from the river and the tides.

Gullah communities were established on the sea islands by freed slaves after the Civil War. Many of them were fishermen who made their living and provided food for their families fishing the rivers and creeks in the low country.

Gullah women pick shrimp caught on the river at low tide.

Bridge Fishing

Gullah fishermen used their skills on the water to provide food for their families and to prepare traditional recipes such as fried fish, stewed shrimp, oyster dressing, and boiled crabs.

Gullah women used hand lines with baskets to catch blue crabs using fish heads, chicken necks and other bait to attract them.

Going Home

Long Day on the River

Gullah fishermen made their own cast nets and went into the creeks and rivers to catch shrimp. Throwing a cast net is an acquired skill and learning how to use it was passed down from one generation to another.

Gullah fishermen digging for Clams.

Shrimping on the May River.

Gullah crabbers pull up a crab trap loaded with Crabs.

Gullah fisherman going out at low tide to catch Shrimp with his cast net. At night he will go out to cast his net for Mullet. When he comes back from the river, he will have enough Shrimp and Mullet to sell and to provide food for his family.

Casting for Shrimp in the Creek.

Gullah Faith and Folk Tales

The New Testament (De Nyew Testament) in Gullah Sea Island Creole with marginal text of the King James Version was completed after 26 years of translating and was introduced at the Heritage Days Festival on St. Helena Island, SC, on November 12, 2005.

"Fa de fus time, God taak to me de way I taak."

Translation: For the first time, God talks to me the way I talk.

After 1845 many plantations had crude structures where slaves could "hold prays" on weekday evenings as well as on Sundays. They could relate their experiences, express their deepest feelings and longings, and celebrate their religion. Usually run by black elders, the Praise House gave the old and respected a place where they could discipline the young, mold their ideology and character, and impart the lore and traditions of a people. For the Gullahs it was an ideal culture medium for transmitting not only Christianity but what had been retained from Africa.

Today the descendants of the Gullah continue to have a spiritual life that influences every aspect of their lives. They believe in the dual nature of the soul and spirit. In death, one's soul returns to God but the spirit remains on earth living among the individual's descendants and participated in their daily affairs such as protecting them and guiding them through spiritual forces.

GULLAH FOLK TALES

Brer Lion an Brer Goat

Brer Lion bin a hunt, an eh spy Brer Goat duh leddown topper er big rock duh wuk eh mout an der chaw. Eh creep up fuh ketch um. Wen eh git close ter um eh notus um good. Brer Goat keep on chaw. Brer Lion try fuh fine out wuh Brer Goat duh eat. Eh yent see nuttne nigh um ceptin de nekked rock wuh eh duh leddown on. Brer Lion stonish. Eh wait topper Brer Goat. Brer Goat keep on chaw, an chaw, an chaw. Brer Lion cant mek de ting out, an eh come close, an eh say: "Hay! Brer Goat, wuh you duh eat?" Brer Goat skade wen Brer Lion rise up befo um, but eh keep er bole harte, an eh mek ansur: "Me duh chaw dis rock, an ef you dont leff, wen me done long um me guine eat you." Dis big wud sabe Brer Goat. Bole man git outer diffikelty way coward man lose eh life.

Translation: *Brer Lion was hunting, and he spied Brer Goat lying down on top of a big rock working his mouth and chewing. He crept up to catch him. When he got close to him, he watched him good. Brer Goat kept on chewing. Brer Lion tried to find out what Brer Goat was eating. He didn't see anything near him except the naked rock which he was lying down on. Brer Lion was astonished. He waited for Brer Goat. Brer Goat kept on chewing, and chewing, and chewing. Brer Lion couldn't make the thing out, and he came close, and he said: "Hey! Brer Goat, what are you eating?" Brer Goat was scared when Brer Lion rose up before him, but he kept a bold heart, and he made (his) answer: "I am chewing this rock, and if you don't leave me (alone), when I am done with it I will eat you." This big word saved Brer Goat. A bold man gets out of difficulty where a cowardly man loses his life.*

Buh Rabbit An De Groun-Mole

Day nebber bin a man wuh kin equel Buh Rabbit fuh mek plan fuh lib offer tarruh people bedout wuk isself. Groun-mole, bin berry tick. On ebry side dem bin er root up de tetter patch, and stroy pinder. No body know how fuh ketch um, case eh wuk onder de groun, and wen you go fuh fine um eh yent dedday.

Buh Rabbit, him see eh chance, an eh tell ebry body him know how fuh stroy um. De ting come ter Buh Wolf yez, an eh sen fuh Buh Rabbit. Buh Rabbit gone ter Buh Wolf, an eh tell um yes, him hab plan fuh clear de fiel er Groun-mole, an dat him wunt charge Buh Wolf nuttne but him boad and lodgment wile him duh ketch an kill de Groun-mole. Buh Wolf him say Buh Rabbit berry kine, an eh gree fuh fine um. Den Buh Wolf hab one nice bed mek up fuh Buh Rabbit, and eh tell eh wife fuh feed um well.

Buh Wolf hab some bidness wuh call um way from home, an eh spec fuh gone bout one week. Eh leff Buh Rabbit fuh clean de Groun-mole outer eh fiel, an den eh gone. Buh Rabbit, him well saterfy. Ebry mornin, arter brukwus, eh mobe off luk eh bin gwine ter Buh Wolf fiel, an nobody shum tel dinner time. Arter eh done eat er hebby dinner, eh gone ger tel supper time, wen eh come back an eat er hebby supper, an den eh leddown der bed. Nobody kin see any Groun-mole wuh Buh Rabbit der ketch, but eh tell Buh Wolf wife dat eh bin er kill heap er dem ebry day, an dat eh gwine soon clear de fiel. De ting gone on dis way tel Buh Wolf tun home. Wen eh retch eh house eh quire bout Buh Rabbit, an eh wife tell um wuh Buh Rabbit bin er say an er do, an dat Buh Rabbit gone der fiel dist arter brukwus. Buh Wolf say him gwine see fuh ehself wuh Buh Rabbit duh do, an wuh plan eh fix fuh ketch de Groun-mole.

Wen eh git der fiel eh look up an down, an eh yent see no sign er Buh Rabbit. Eh notus eh crap, an de Groun-mole duh eat um wus den nebber. Eh sarche fuh Buh Rabbit track, an eh cant shum no way. Buh Wolf mek up eh mine dat Buh Rabbit yent do de fus ting een de fiel. De sun hot. Buh Wolf gone een de edge er de wood, an day eh come pon topper Buh Rabbit tretch out een er bed wuh eh bin mek outer pine straw onder one tree, fas tersleep. Eh yent bin study bout Buh Wolf, er de Groun-mole wuh bin er bodder de fiel. Buh Wolf slip up, and eh graff um tight. Buh Rabbit so skade eh furgit fuh lie, anBuh Wolf mek um confess eh yent know how fuh ketch Groun-mole, dat eh nebber did kill none, an dat eh bin lib offer Buh Wolf bittle ebber sence eh leff.

Buh Wolf, him so be eh git grape wine an eh tie Buh Rabbit han an foot, an eh lick um tel eh tired. All dis time Buh Rabbit bin er holler an er bague. At lenk Buh Wolf loose um, an run um offer de place.

Eh yent often Buh Rabbit ketch at him trick, but eh meet eh match dis time.

BUH TUKREY BUZZUD AN DE RAIN

Buh Tukrey Buzzud, him yent hab no sense no how. You watch um. Wen do rain duh po down, eh set on de fench an eh aquinch up isself. Eh draw in eh neck, an eh try fur hide eh head, an eh look dat pittyful you rale sorry for um. Eh duh half cry, an eh say to isself: "Nummine, wen dis rain ober me guine buil house right off. Me yent guine leh dis rain lick me dis way no mo."

Wen de rain done gone, an de win blow, an de sun shine, wuh buh Tukrey Buzzud do? Eh set on de top er de dead pine ree way di sun kin wam um, an eh retch out eh wing, an eh tun roun an roun so de win kin dry eh fedder, an eh laugh to isself, an eh say: "Dis rain done ober. Eh yent guine rain no mo. No use fur me fuh buil house now." Caless man dis like Buh Tukrey Buzzud.

DE EAGLE AN EH CHILLUN

De Eagle, him duh er wise bud. Eh mek en nes on one tall pine tree close de ribber, er de sea, way nuttne kin git at um. Eh saterfy wide two chillun.Eh tek good care er um. Ebry hour eh fetch um snake an fish, an eh garde um from win an rain an fowl-hawk, an mek um grow fas. Wen eh wing kibber wid fedder an eh strong nough fur fly, whu Buh Eagle do? Eh wint leff dem chillun een de nes fuh lazy an lib pontopper eh farruh an eh murrer, but eh tek um on eh wing, an eh sail ober de sea, an eh tell eh chillun: "De time come fuh you fuh mek you own libbin. Me feed you long nough. Now you haffer look out fuh youself." Wid dat, eh fly from onder dem, an de noung bud, wen eh fine out eh murrer yent gwine cahr um no furder, an dat dem haffer shif fuh demself, dem rtry eh wing an sail off een de element duh hunt bittle.

People orter tek notus er buh Eagle an do jes es him do. Wen you chillun git big nough fuh wuk, mek um wuk. Dont leh um set bout de house duh do nuttne, an duh spek eh farruh an eh murrer fuh fine bittle an cloze fuh um. Ef you does, you chillun gwine mek you shame, an eh will tun out berry triflin. Eh will keep you dead po, too.

Do same luk buh Eagle. Mine you chillun well wen dem leetle; an soon dem big nough fuh wuk, mek um wuk.

BUH ROCCOON AN BUH POSSUM

Buh Roccoon ax Buh Possum wuh mek, wen de dog tackle um, eh double up ehself, an kibber eh yeye wid eh han, an wunt fight lucker man an lick de dog off. Buh Possum grin eh teet same lucker fool, an eh say, wen de dog come pon topper um, dem tickle him rib so bad long demmout dat him bleege ter laugh; an so him furgit fuh fight.

Gullah Superstitions

Superstitions are plentiful in the Gullah culture. Here are a few of the more familiar ones:

1. If bubbles form on top of your coffee, you will get money soon.

2. Rheumatism can be cured by carrying an Irish (white) potato in your pocket.

3. When you hear a screech owl, it's a sure sign of death.

4. Never throw your hair outside because it is a part of your personal body and someone could use it to put a "fix" on you.

5. If a dog howls outside, it's a sign that somebody is dead or dying.

6. It is bad luck to sweep after sundown because you'll sweep yourself out of a home. This superstition may also be based on the African belief that the good spirits come into the house at night and may be swept out by mistake along with the dust.

7. The Gullahs dressed graves with life's necessities and pleasures so the departed could pass easily and amiably between material and spiritual worlds: a cup of water for thirst, a jar of rice for hunger, a lantern for light, a wooden pistol for protection, a bed frame for rest, herbs for health. They regarded cemeteries as sacred ground and left them alone.

8. They painted houses blue to banish evil spirits and tossed salt to get rid of unwanted guests. They also painted some rooms inside blue to keep out spirits, called hags, during childbirth.

9. Long ago a Gullah root doctor might have advised a friend with high blood pressure to tuck a little moss into the shoe sole, or to dress a wound with cobwebs to stop bleeding, or to brew holly berry tea to ease pain.

Gullah Folklore
Hags, Witches and Hants

Hags and hants are a part of Gullah Folklore. Most folks believe that hags are witches who live normal lives during the day. But, at night they shed their skin and go out to "ride" folks in their sleep. It is a common belief that hags spend their nights "riding" people. This means that they sit on the chest of their victims and make them have nightmares. Some say that they suck up the victim's voice so that she can't scream or call out to anyone. A few people claim to have actually touched a hag. Those who have touched a hag describe the sensation as "touching warm raw meat."

Stories of skin-shedding hags probably have their beginnings in the West Indies where the people believe that hags and witches shed their skins after midnight and travel around at will. Another carryover from the West Indies is that the hag is part witch and part vampire. She can fly and she can suck blood. One old man said: "Dey goes in en sucks your blood troo yer nose."

Another superstition is that a hag won't cross your doorsill if you put a broom across it. Some say that the hag will not only try to count the straws in the broom, but she will also try to measure the length of each one. Therefore, a broom might keep the old hag too busy to notice that the sun is coming up and she'll get caught. Hags can't stand sunlight or salt so they always leave the victim's house before the sun rises and return to their bodies.

Haunts or hants as the Gullah call them are more powerful than hags. As spirits of the dead they can walk right through barred doors and walls. They are most likely to be seen when the moon is full and they make strange things happen in the house like lifting the lid of a jar or causing a rocking chair to rock without anyone sitting in it. They will do anything to scare the occupant of the house. Haints are everywhere but they seem to prefer graveyards and swamps.

Gullah Customs and Traditions

*African influences are found in every aspect
of the Gullahs' traditional way of life.*

---Gullah word "Guber" for peanut derives straight from Kongo (Congo) word "N'guba"

---Gullah rice dishes called "red rice" and "okra soup" are similar to West African "jollof rice" and "okra soup". Jollof rice is a style of cooking brought by the Wolof and Mande peoples of West Africa.

---The Gullah version of "gumbo" has its roots in African cooking. "Gumbo" is derived from a word in the Umbundu language of Angola, meaning "okra."

---Gullah rice farmers once used the mortar and pestle and "fanner" (winnowing basket) similar to tools used by West African rice farmers.

---Gullah beliefs about "hags", "haunts" and "plat-eyes" are similar to African beliefs about malevolent ancestors, witches, and "devils" (forest spirits).

---Gullah "root doctors" protect their clients against dangerous spiritual forces using similar ritual objects to those employed by African medicine men.

---Gullah herbal medicines are similar to traditional African remedies.

---The Gullah "seekin" ritual is similar to coming of age ceremonies in West African secret societies like Poro and Sande.

---Gullah spirituals, shouts, and other musical forms employ the "call and response" method commonly used in African music.

---Gullah "sweetgrass baskets" are almost identical to coil baskets made by the Wolof people in Senegal.

---The folk song Michael Row the Boat Ashore (or Michael Row Your Boat Ashore) comes from the Gullah culture.

Glossary of Gullah Language

Abnue - avenue.
Agg - egg.
An - and.
arter - after.
Arur - each, either.
Ax - ask

Bactize - baptize.
Bague - to beg.
Barruh - barrow.
Beber - beaver.
Bedout - without.
Ben - bend, bent, been.
Berry - very.
Bes - best.
Bex - vex, vexed.
Bidness - business.
Biggin - begin, began.
Bimeby - by and by, presently.
Binner - was, were.
Bittle - victuals.
Blan - in the habit of, accustomed to.
Blanks - belongs to.
Bleebe - believe.
Bieege - obliged, compelled.
Bodder - to bother.
Bode - board, boards.
Bofe - both.
Bole - bold.
Boun - resolved upon,forced to.
Bredder - brother.
Bref - breath.
Bres - breast.
Bresh - brush-wood, to brush.
Broke up - to leave, to depart.
Brukwus - breakfast.
Buckra - white man.
Bud - bird.

Budduh - brother.
Bun - burn.
Buss - burst, or break through.

Cahr - carry.
Caze - because.
Ceive - deceive.
Cept - accept, accepted, except.
Chillun - children.
Chimbly - chimmey.
Chune - tune.
Cist - insist.
Clorte - cloth.
Cloze - clothes.
Cohoot - bargain, agreement.
Cole - cold.
Conjunct - agree to, conclude.
Cote - court.
Crack eh teet - make answer.
Crap - crop.
Crape - scrape.
Cratch - scratch.
Cut down - disappointed, chagrined.

Darter - daughter.
Day - there, is, to be, am.
Day day - to be there.
Den - then.
Der - was, were, into.
Dest - just, only.
Destant - distant, distance.
Det - death.
Diffunce - difference.
Disher - this.
Do - door.
Dout - without.
Drap - drop, dropped.
Duh - was, were.

Glossary of Gullah Language

Dunno - don't know.
Dut - dirt.

Edder - other.
Eeben - even.
Een - in, end.
Eenwite - invite.
Ef - if.
Eh - he, she, it, his, her, its.
Enty - are you not, are they not,
    do you not, do they not, is it
    not.

Faber - favor.
Faid - to be afraid.
Fambly - family.
Fanner - a shallow basket.
Farruh, Farrur - father.
Feber - fever.
Fedder - feather, feathers.
Fiel - field
Fine - supply with food, find.
Flaber - flavor.
Flo - floor.
Flut - flirt.
Foce - force.
Forrud - forehead.
Fren - friend.
Fros - frost.
Fuh - for.
Fuh sutten - for a certainty.
Fuss - first.

Gage - engage.
Gedder - gather, collect.
Gelt - to girt.
Gem - to give.
Gen - gave, again.
Gie - give.
Gimme - give me.
Glec - neglect.

Glub - gloves.
Gooly - good.
Graff - grab.
Gree - agree, consent.
Grine salt - fly round and round.
Guine, Gwine - going, going to.

Haffer - have to, had to.
Hair rise - badly frightened.
Haky, Harky - hearken to, heed.
Han - hand.
Hanker - long for, desire.
Hatchich - hatchet.
Head - get the better of.
Head um - get ahead of him.
Hebby - heavy.
Holler - halloo, hollow.
Honna - you.
Hot - to hurt.
Huccum - how happens it, why,
              how come.
Huddy - how d 'ye do.

Ile me bade - grease my mouth.
Isself - himself, herself, itself,
            themselves.

Jew - dew.
Jist - just.
Juk - jerk.

Ketch - catch, reach to, approach.
Kibber - cover.
Kine - kind.
Knowledge - acknowledge, admit.

Labuh - labor.
Lass - to suffice for, to last.
Lean fuh - set out for.
Led - dow - lay down.
Leek - to lick with the tongue.

Glossary of Gullah Language

Leely, Leetle - little.
Leff - to leave, did leave, left.
Leggo - to let go.
Leh - let.
Lemme - let me.
Lenk - length.
Libbin - living.
Lick - to whip, stroke of the whip.
Lickin - whipping.
Lick back - turn rapidly back.
Lief - leave, permission.
Light on - to mount.
Light out - to start off.
Long - with, from.
Lub - love.
Luk, lucker - like.

Mange - mane.
Medjuh - measure.
Mek - Make, made.
Mek fuh - to go to.
Mek out - fare, thrive, succeed.
Member - to remind.
Men eh pace - increase his speed.
Mine - mind, heed, take care of.
Miration - wonder, astonishment.
Mo - more.
Moober - moreover.
Mona, moner - more than.
Most - almost.
Mossa - master.
Mouf, Mout - mouth.
Murrer - mother.
Mussne - must not.
Muster - must have.

Nabor - neighbor.
Narruh - another.
Nebber - never.
Nekked - naked.
Nes - nest.

Nigh - to draw near to.
Notus - notice, observe.
Noung - young.
Nudder - another.
Nuff - enough.
Nummine - never mind.
Nurrer - neither, another.
Nuse - use, employ.
Nussen - used to, accustomed to.
Nuss - nurse.
Nuttne - nothing.

Obersheer - overseer.
Offer - off of.
Ole - old.
Ooman - woman, women.
Out - to go out, to extinguish.
Outer - out of.

Pahler - parlor.
Passon - parson.
Pate - path.
Pen pon - depend upon.
Perwision - provisions.
Pinder - ground-nuts, peanuts.
Pint - direct, directed, point.
Pintment - appointment.
Pit - put, apply.
Playpossum - to fool, to practice
                deceit.
Pledjuh - pleasure.
Po - poor, pour.
Pon, upon.
Pooty, pretty.
Pose, post.
Prommus - promise.
Pruppus - on purpose.
Pusson - person.

Quaintun - acquainted with.
Quaintunce - acquaintances.

Glossary of Gullah Language

Quile - to coil, coiled.
Quire - to inquire, inquired.

Rale - very, truly, really.
Range - reins.
Rastle - to wrestle.
Retch - to reach, to arrive at.
Ribber - river.
Riz - rose.
Roose - roost.

Sabe - to know.
San - sand.
Sarbis - service, kindness.
Satify - satisfied, content, happy.
Scace - scarce.
Schway - to swear, swore.
Scuse - excuse.
Seaznin - seasoning.
Sebbn - seven
Sed - sit, sat.
Sed-down - sit down, sat down.
Shet - shut.
Sho - sure.
Sholy - surely.
Shum - to see it, see him, see her, see them.
Sider - on the side of.
Sisso - say so.
Skade - scared.
Smate - smart.
Sofe - soft.
Soon man - very smart, wide-awake man.
Sorter - sort of, after a fashion.
Sparruh - sparrow.
Spec - expect.
Spose - expose.
Spute - contest the championship with.
State - start, begin.

Steader, Stidder - instead of.
Straighten fur - run rapidly for.
Stroy - destroy.
Sukkle - circle, fly around.
Summuch - so much.
Sutten - certain, sudden.
Suttenly - certainly, suddenly.
Swade, persuade.
Swode - sword.

Tack - to attack.
Tackie - to hold to account.
Tan - to stand.
Tarrify - to terrify, to annoy.
Tarruh, Turruh - the other.
Tase - to taste, taste.
Tay - stay.
Tek - take.
Tek wid um - pleased with him, her, or it.
Tek you foot - to walk.
Tel - until.
Ten - attend to.
Tend - intend.
Tenk, Tenky - to thank, thanks.
Tetch - to touch.
Tetter - potatoes.
Tick - thick, abundant, a stick.
Ticket - thicket.
Tickler - particular.
Tief - to steal, thief.
Ting - thing.
Tird - third.
Titter - sister.
Togerruh - together.
Tole - Told
Topper - on top of, on.
Tote - carry.
Trabble - travel.
Tru - through.
Truss - trust.

Glossary of Gullah Language

Trute - truth.
Tuff - tuft.
Tuk - took.
Tun - turn, return.
Tun flour - to cook hominy.

Up ter de notch - in the best style.
Usen - to be in the habit of.

Vise - to advise.
Vive - revive.

Wan - to want, to wish, want.
Warse - wasp.
Wase - waste.
Way - where.
Wayebber - wherever.
Whalin ob er - enormous, severe.
Wid - with.
Wile - while.
Win - Wind.
Wine - vine.
Wish de time er day - to say goodby,
                         how d 'ye do.
Wud - word.
Wudduh dat - what is that.
Wuffer - what for, why, what to.
Wuh - what, which,who.
Wuhebber -whatever.
Wuk - work.
Wul - world.
Wunt - will not, would not.
Wurrum - worms.
Wus - worse.
Wus den nebber - worse than ever.
Wut, worth.

Yad, yard.
Yearin - hearing.
Yeddy - to hear, to hearken to.

Yent day day - is not there, are not
                         there.
Yeye - eye, eyes.
Yez - ear, ears.
Yiz - am, is, to be, did.
Yuh - here.

Zamine - examine.

NUMBERS

One - one.
Two - two.
Tree - three.
Fo - four.
Fibe - five.
Six - six.
Sebbn - seven.
Eight - eight.
Nine - nine.
Ten - ten.
Lebbn - eleven.
Twelbe - twelve.
Tirteen - thirteen.
Foteen - fourteen.
Fifteen - fifteen.
Sixteen - sisteen.
Sebbnteen - seventeen.
Eighteen - eighteen.
Nineteen - nineteen.
Twenty - twenty.
Tirty - thirty.
Forty - forty.
Fifty - fifty.
Sixty - sixty.
Sebbnty - seventy.
Eighty - eighty.
Ninety - ninety.
One hundud - one hundred.

Glossary of Gullah Language

Trute - truth.
Tuff - tuft.
Tuk - took.
Tun - turn, return.
Tun flour - to cook hominy.

Up ter de notch - in the best style.
Usen - to be in the habit of.

Vise - to advise.
Vive - revive.

Wan - to want, to wish, want.
Warse - wasp.
Wase - waste.
Way - where.
Wayebber - wherever.
Whalin ob er - enormous, severe.
Wid - with.
Wile - while.
Win - Wind.
Wine - vine.
Wish de time er day - to say goodby,
                          how d 'ye do.
Wud - word.
Wudduh dat - what is that.
Wuffer - what for, why, what to.
Wuh - what, which,who.
Wuhebber -whatever.
Wuk - work.
Wul - world.
Wunt - will not, would not.
Wurrum - worms.
Wus - worse.
Wus den nebber - worse than ever.
Wut, worth.

Yad, yard.
Yearin - hearing.
Yeddy - to hear, to hearken to.
Yender -is not, are not, did not.

Yent day day - is not there, are not
                          there.
Yeye - eye, eyes.
Yez - ear, ears.
Yiz - am, is, to be, did.
Yuh - here.

Zamine - examine.

NUMBERS

One - one.
Two - two.
Tree - three.
Fo - four.
Fibe - five.
Six - six.
Sebbn - seven.
Eight - eight.
Nine - nine.
Ten - ten.
Lebbn - eleven.
Twelbe - twelve.
Tirteen - thirteen.
Foteen - fourteen.
Fifteen - fifteen.
Sixteen - sisteen.
Sebbnteen - seventeen.
Eighteen - eighteen.
Nineteen - nineteen.
Twenty - twenty.
Tirty - thirty.
Forty - forty.
Fifty - fifty.
Sixty - sixty.
Sebbnty - seventy.
Eighty - eighty.
Ninety - ninety.
One hundud - one hundred.
One tousan - one thousand.

Glossary of Gullah Language

MONTHS OF THE YEAR

Jinnywerry - January.
Febbywerry - February.
Mache - March.
Aprul - April.
May - May.
June - June.
Jully - July.
Augus - August.
Sectember - September.
October - October.
November - November.
December - December.

DAYS OF THE WEEK

Mundy - Monday.
Chuseday - Tuesday.
Wensday - Wednesday.
Tursday - Thursday.
Friday - Friday.
Sattyday - Saturday.
Sunday - Sunday.

Glossary of Art by Pearce W. Hammond

Glossary of Art by Pearce W. Hammond

Bibliography

Branch, Muriel M. *The Water Brought us*. New York, NY: Cobblehill Books, 1995.

Conroy, Pat. *The Water is Wide*. Boston, MA: Houghton Mifflin, 1972.

Jones, Charles C., Jr. *Negro Myths from the Georgia Coast,* Told in the Vernacular. Boston: Houghton, Mifflin,1888.

Geraty, Virginia M., *Gullah For You*. Orangeburg, SC: Sandlapper Publishing Co. Inc., 1997.

McFeely, William S. *Sapelo's People*. New York, NY: W.W. Norton & Co., Inc., 1994.

Pollitzer, William S. *The Gullah People and Their African Heritage*. Athens, GA: University of Georgia Press, 1999.

Carawan, Guy and Candie. *Ain't you got a right to the tree of life?* Athens, GA: The University of Georgia Press, 1989.

Turner, Lorenzo D. *Africanisms in the Gullah Dialect*. Columbia, SC.: University of South Carolina Press, 1969.

Chase, Judith W. *Afro-American Art and Craft*. New York: Van Nostrand, 1971.

Crum, Mason. Gullah: *Negro Life in the Carolina Sea Islands*. New York: Negro Universities Press, 1968.

Jones, Katherine M. *Port Royal Under Six Flags*. Indianapolis: Bobbs-Merrill, 1960.

Kovacik, Charles F. *South Carolina: A Geography*. Boulder, CO: Westview Press, 1987.

Parrish, Lydia. *Slave Songs of the Georgia Sea Islands*. Athens, GA: University of Georgia Press, 1992.

Woofter, T.J. Black Yeomanry: *Life on St. Helena Island*. New York: Henry Holt, 1930.

Joyner, Charles W. *Down by the Riverside*. Urbanna: University of Illinois Press, 1984.

Hamilton, Virginia. *The People Could Fly: American Black Folktales*. New York: Knopf, 1985.

NOTES

NOTES

Made in the USA
Charleston, SC
22 July 2011